OPEN COURT READING

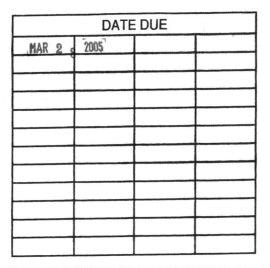

DATE DUE

MAR 2 9 2005			

e:

ition

SRA

A Division of The McGraw·Hill Companies

Columbus, Ohio

www.sra4kids.com

SRA/McGraw-Hill

*A Division of The **McGraw·Hill** Companies*

Copyright © 2002 by SRA/McGraw-Hill.

Send all inquiries to:
SRA/McGraw-Hill
8787 Orion Place
Columbus, OH 43240-4027

Printed in the United States of America.

ISBN 0-07-572050-7

  2 3 4 5 6 7 8 9 QPD 07 06 05 04 03 02

Table of Contents

▶Identifying Letters

Directions: Color yellow the boxes with *Aa*. Color orange the boxes with *Bb*.

O	A [Y]	d	e	b [O]	f
C	X	B [O]	k	T	B [O]
A [Y]	a [Y]	p	a [Y]	L	N
b [O]	U	w	E	B [O]	u

PHONICS SKILLS

UNIT 1 Let's Read! • **Lesson 2** *The Purple Cow*

▶Identifying Letters

PHONICS SKILLS

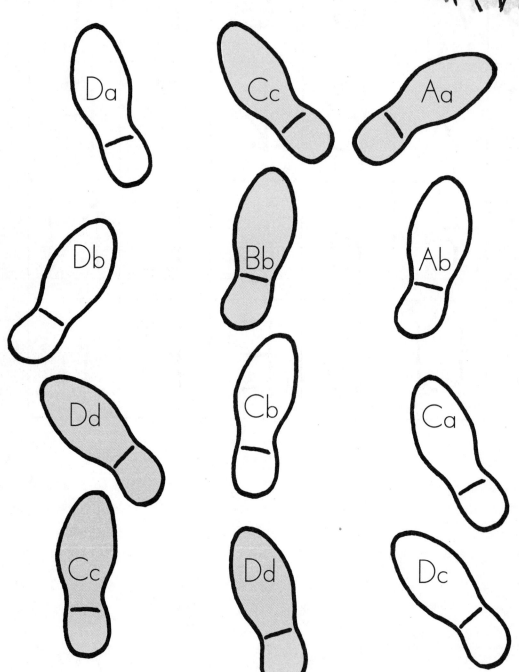

Identifying Letters • Challenge: Phonics Skills

Name ______________________ Date __________

Identifying Letters

Directions: Trace the lowercase letter that matches the capital letter given on each line.

E	a	p	v	e
F	d	f	q	y
G	w	g	n	r

PHONICS SKILLS

▶Identifying Letters

Directions: Color the road that has only *Hh*, *Ii*, and *Jj* to lead the horse back to the field.

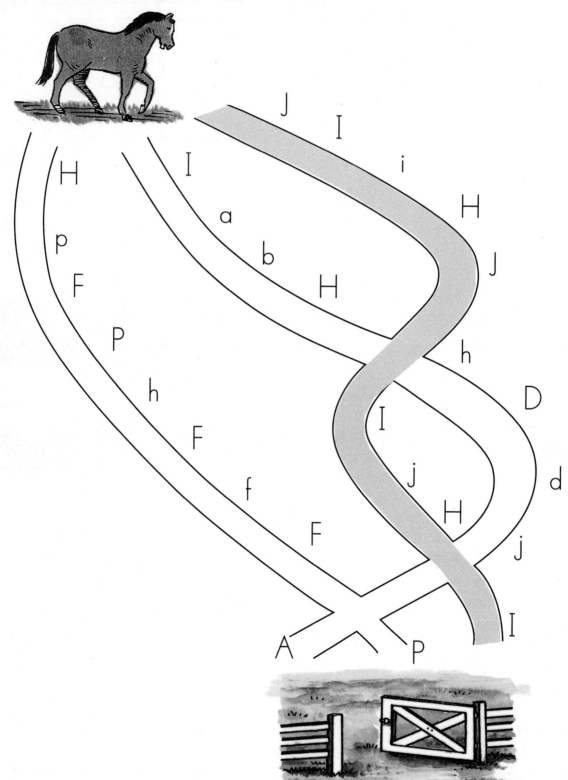

Identifying Letters • **Challenge: Phonics Skills**

▶Identifying Letters

Directions: Circle the capital and lowercase letters that match the letter at the beginning of the row.

PHONICS SKILLS

K   a (K) E (k)

L   b (L I) A

M   (m) h (M) D

▶Identifying Letters

Directions: Color all the boxes that have Nn, Oo, and Pp.

PHONICS SKILLS

g	B	o	f	P
w	r	N	m	e
q	P	o	u	r
B	G	n	W	P
R	O	r	N	n

UNIT I   Let's Read! • **Lesson 7** *Rain*

▶Identifying Letters

Directions: Color matching pairs of capital and lowercase letters.

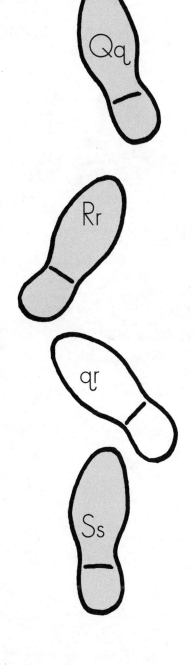

Qq   Qr   Rs

Rr   Sr   Ss

qr   sq   Qq

Ss   Rr   Rq

PHONICS SKILLS

Challenge: Phonics Skills • *Identifying Letters*

▶Identifying Letters

Directions: Find all the Tt, Uu, and Vv and circle them.

UNIT 1 Let's Read! • **Lesson 9** *Rags*

▶ Identifying Letters

Directions: Color all the Ww and Xx to find the hidden picture.

PHONICS SKILLS

▶Identifying Letters

Directions: Color all the Yy green and the Zz black.

PHONICS SKILLS

A

Z
[B]

a

w

V

d

Y
[G]

F

Z
[B]

y
[G]

C

P

t

Y
[G]

z
[B]

y
[G]

UNIT 1   Let's Read! • **Lesson 10** *Twinkle Twinkle Firefly*

▶Capital and Lowercase Letters

Directions: Draw a line between the capital and lowercase letter pairs that go together.

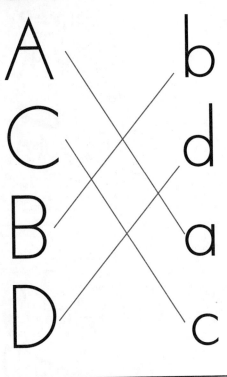

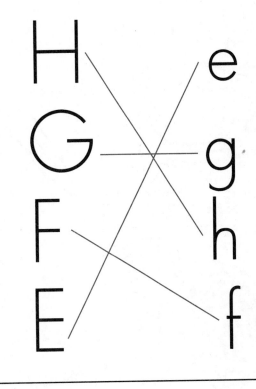

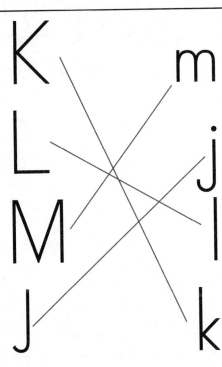

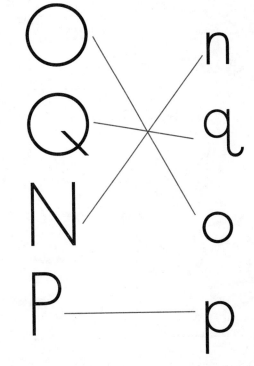

▶Sounds and Spelling

PHONICS SKILLS

[color]

[color]

[color]

[color]

[color]

UNIT 1 Let's Read! • **Lesson 12** *The Chase*

▶ Sounds and Spelling

Directions: Color the pictures red that begin with the /m/ sound. Color the pictures yellow that end with the /m/ sound.

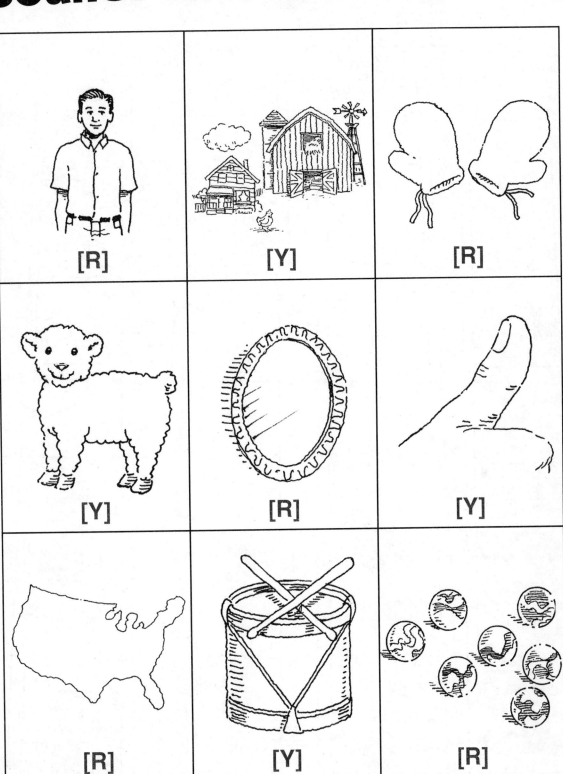

[R]	[Y]	[R]
[Y]	[R]	[Y]
[R]	[Y]	[R]

PHONICS SKILLS

▶ Sounds and Spelling

Directions: Circle the ladder in which all words contain the /a/ sound.

and	on	am	and
an	is	an	an
in	in	is	am
Mom	an	and	Sam

▶ Sounds and Spellings

Directions: Color in the spaces with words that contain the /t/ sound to find the hidden picture.

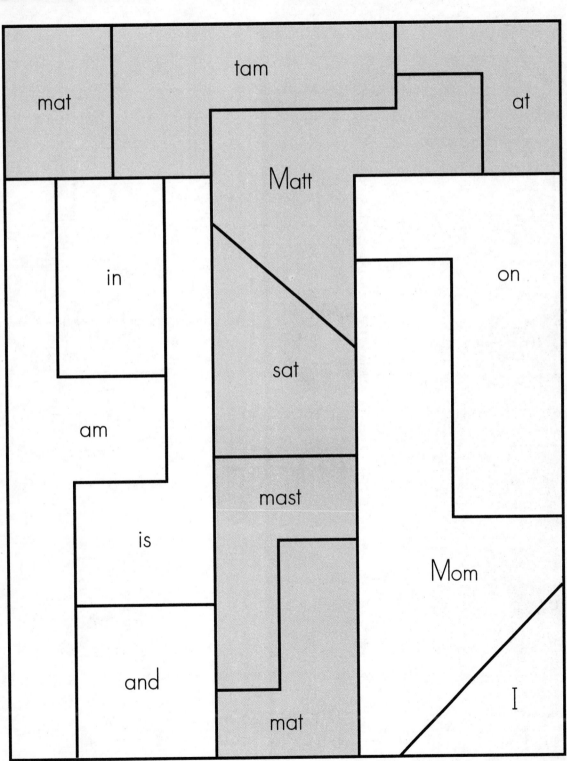

PHONICS SKILLS

▶ Sounds and Spellings

PHONICS SKILLS

h

t

m

t

m

h

m

t

h

▶ Sounds and Spelling

| map | tap | stamp | Pam |

map

stamp

Pam

tap

Pam has a stamp.
Pam taps the map.

Pam has a stamp.

Challenge: Phonics Skills • *Sounds and Spelling*   UNIT 2 • Lesson 1   **17**

PHONICS SKILLS

PHONICS SKILLS

►Vowel Sounds and Spelling

Directions: Write the word that matches each picture. The letters in the shaded boxes form another word. Write it on the line.

| sit | spin | pit | hit |

tips

Name _____   Date _____

▶ Consonant Sounds and Spelling

Directions: Circle the items that have the /n/ sound.

PHONICS SKILLS

[sun]

[pants]

[pin]

[Nat]

[bench]

[sand]

[ants]

▶ Consonant Sounds and Spelling

PHONICS SKILLS

hill	lips	fall	lamp

lips

lamp

fall

hill

Sentence will vary.

_____

UNIT 2 Animals • **Lesson 5** *Baby Animals*

▶Review

Directions: Circle the items that have the /l/, /n/, /p/, or /i/ sounds.

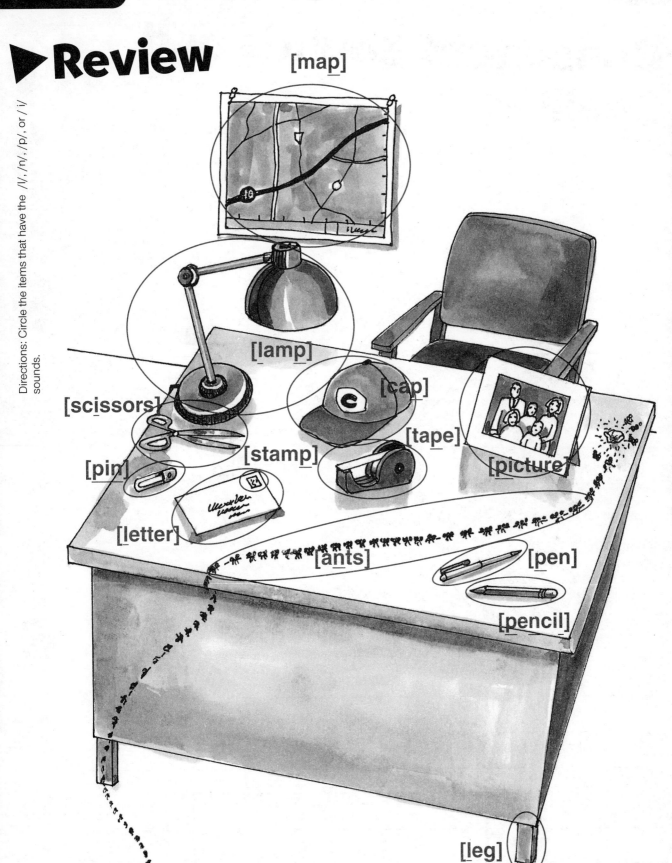

[map]

[lamp]

[scissors]

[cap]

[tape]

[picture]

[pin]

[stamp]

[letter]

[ants]

[pen]

[pencil]

[leg]

PHONICS SKILLS

UNIT 2 Animals • **Lesson 6** *Munch Crunch*

PHONICS SKILLS

▶ # Consonant Sounds and Spelling

Directions: Draw a line between each picture and the word it matches. Then, write the words on the lines.

Possible answers are shown.

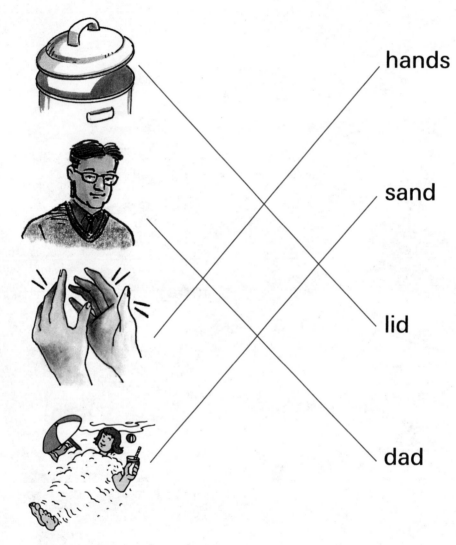

hands

sand

lid

dad

hands   sand

lid   dad

▶ Vowel Sounds and Spelling

Directions: Write a sentence to describe each picture.

Possible answers are shown.

The pot is hot.

Dad has a mop.

I am on top.

It says Stop!

PHONICS SKILLS

Name ________________________________ Date ____________

Consonant Sounds and Spelling

PHONICS SKILLS

Directions: Circle the objects that begin with the /b/ sound.

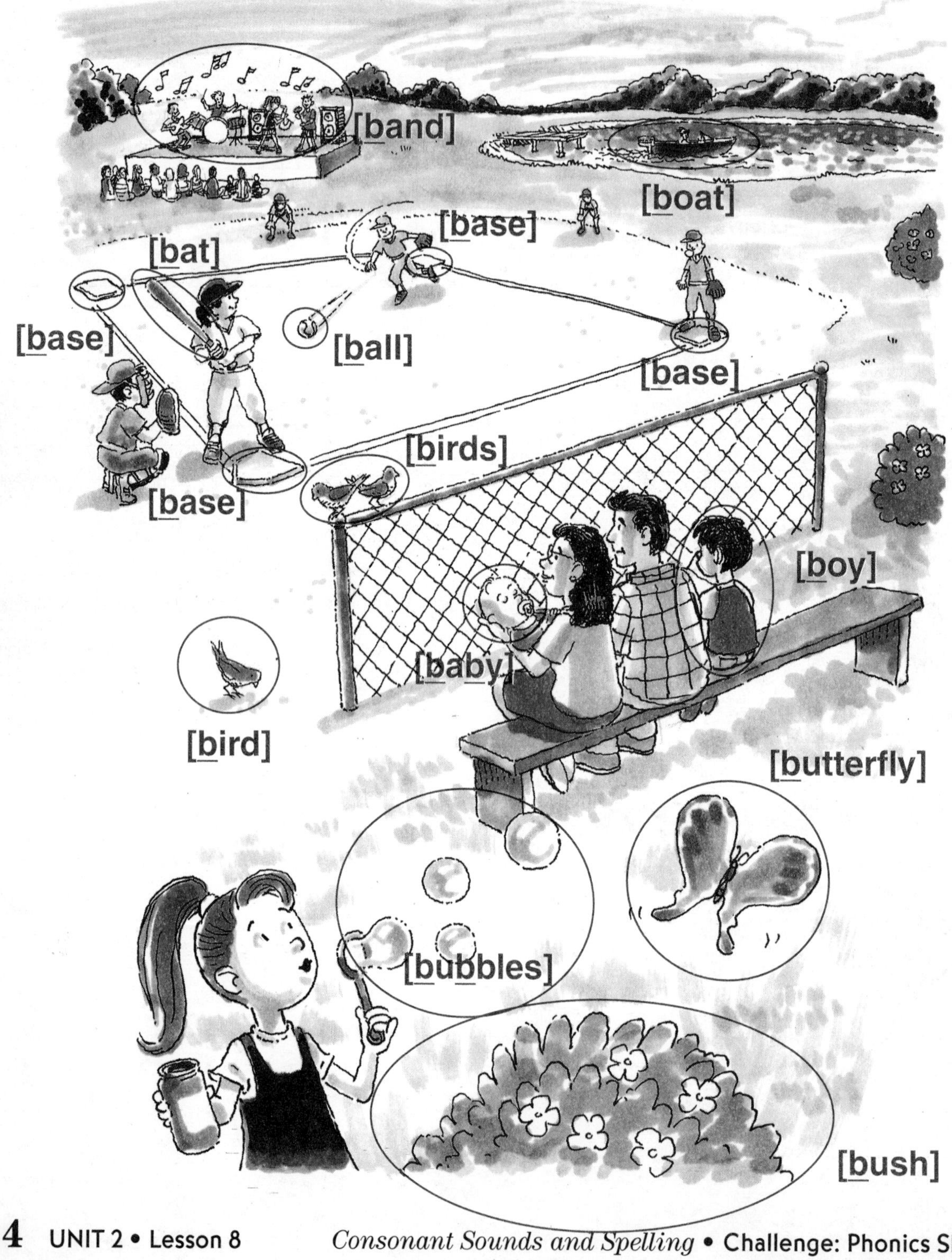
[band]
[boat]
[base]
[bat]
[base]
[ball]
[base]
[birds]
[base]
[boy]
[baby]
[bird]
[butterfly]
[bubbles]
[bush]

Name _____ Date _____

▶ Consonant Sounds and Spelling

Directions: Draw a line between each picture and the word that matches it. Write the words on the line.

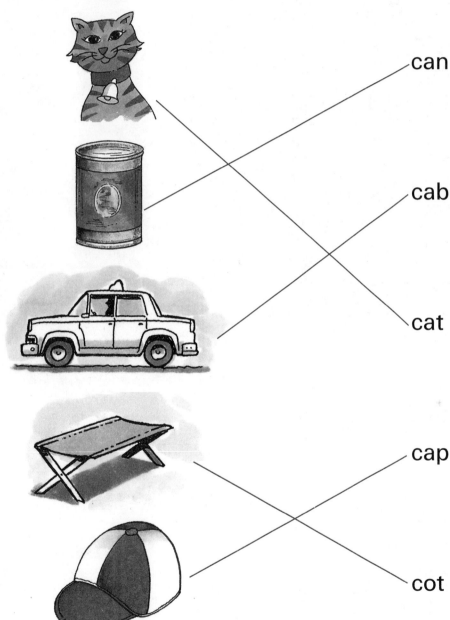

can

cab

cat

cap

cot

PHONICS SKILLS

can cab cat cap cot

▶Review

Directions: Circle the items that have the /d/, /o/, /b/, or /k/ sounds.

PHONICS SKILLS

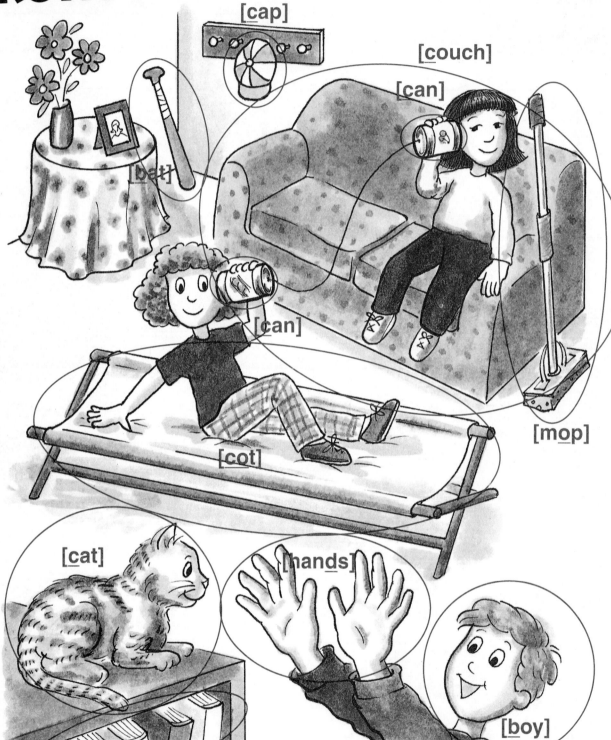

[cap]
[couch]
[can]
[bat]
[can]
[mop]
[cot]
[cat]
[hands]
[boy]
[books]

Review • Challenge: Phonics Skills

UNIT 2 Animals • **Lesson II** *Spiders*

▶ Consonant Sounds and Spelling

Directions: Circle the objects that end in the /k/ sound spelled *ck*

[lock] [dock] [lick] [sock] [duck] [rock] [sack] [stick]

▶Consonant Sounds and Spelling

Directions: Write the word that matches each picture.

| rock | rack | rabbit | ram | rat | ramp |

rabbit

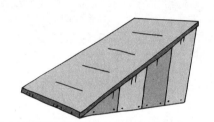

ramp

rock

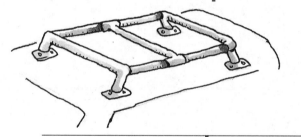

rack

ram

rat

▶Vowel Sounds and Spelling

Directions: Circle the items that have the /u/ sound.

PHONICS SKILLS

[sun]

[mug]

[bus]

[tub]

[truck]

[duck]

[pup]

▶Consonant Sounds and Spelling

Directions: Write the word that matches each picture.

PHONICS SKILLS

| rug | bug | gum | pig | tag | bag |

pig

tag

bag

rug

gum

bug

Consonant Sounds and Spelling • Challenge: Phonics Skills

UNIT 2 Animals • **Lesson 15** *Unit Wrap-Up*

▶Review

Directions: Circle in blue the words that have the /a/ sound, circle in red the words that have the /i/ sound, circle in green the words that have the /o/ sound. Circle in orange the words that have the /u/ sound.

bag
[blue]

hat
[blue]

pig
[red]

truck
[orange]

mug
[orange]

lock
[green]

tag
[blue]

sit
[red]

rat
[blue]

sick
[red]

tug
[orange]

rack
[blue]

rock
[green]

luck
[orange]

sack
[blue]

sock
[green]

PHONICS SKILLS

▶Consonant Sounds and Spelling

Directions: Color all the objects in the picture that have the /j/ sound.

[jet]

[bridge]

[jogger]

[badge]

[jar]

[jacket]

[jug]

[juggler]

[pajamas]

UNIT 3 **Things That Go • Lesson 2** *I Go With My Family to Grandma's*

▶ Sounds and Spelling

sift   raft   fox   gift

Directions: Write the word that matches each picture. The letters in the shaded boxes form another word. Write it on the line.

1.    s i **f** t

2.    **r** a f t

3.    f **o** x

4. 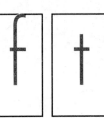   **g** i f t

frog

UNIT 3 · **Things That Go** • **Lesson 3** *I Go With My Family to Grandma's*

▶Vowel Sounds and Spelling

PHONICS SKILLS

[tent]

[web]

[pen]

[desk]

[bed]

[hen]

[eggs]

[nest]

[step]

[sled]

▶Review

Directions: Write the letter that begins the name of each picture.

1.

t

2.

t

3.

b

4.

l

5.

p

6.

p

7.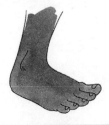

f

8.

m

9.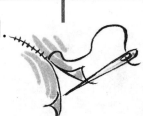

S or n

10.

c

11.

d

12.

l

PHONICS SKILLS

▶Consonant Sounds and Spelling

PHONICS SKILLS

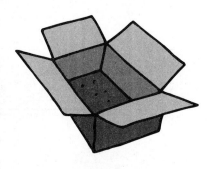

ox   six   box

fox   exit

▶Sounds and Spelling

| bus | jazz | buzz | is | zip |

Directions: Fill in the crossword puzzle by choosing words from the box and using the clues below.

ACROSS →

2.

DOWN ↓

1.

3.

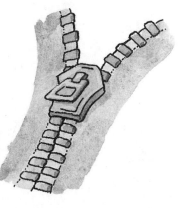

2.

4. Max _____ a dog.

▶Review

Directions: Find all the words from the box in the puzzle and circle them. You will use some letters more than once.

PHONICS SKILLS

fuzz	his	zap	fox
zip	fizz	six	

```
f  r  c  i  t  h  t  l
b  f  a  k  t  z  a  p
h  i  s  r  k  o  l  j
k  z  t  f  u  z  z  l
l  z  p  o  f  l  k  f
s  s  i  x  l  z  i  p
d  p  v  l  o  a  c  o
```

Review • Challenge: Phonics Skills

▶ Consonant Sounds and Spelling

Directions: Circle the objects that contain the /sh/ sound.

[ship]

[shark]

[fresh]

FRESH

[fish]

[fish]

BAIT SHOP

[trash]

[shop]

[shell]

[fish]

[dish]

PHONICS SKILLS

▶ Consonant Sounds and Spelling

Directions: Circle the objects whose names have the /th/ sound.

[<u>th</u>under]

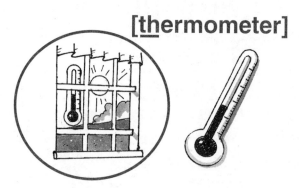
[<u>th</u>read]

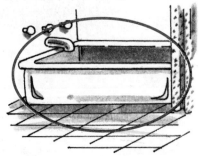
[ba<u>th</u>tub]

[<u>th</u>ermometer]

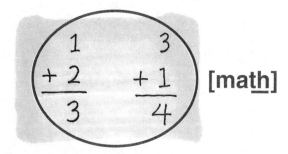
[ma<u>th</u>]

UNIT 3   Things That Go • **Lesson 10** *On the Go*

▶Review

Directions: Color the items that contain the /sh/ sound orange. Color the items that contain the /th/ sound green.

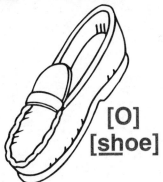

[O]
[sh̲oe]

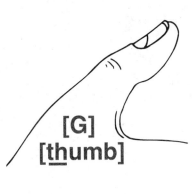

[G]
[t̲humb]

[t̲hread]

[G]

[O]
[sh̲eep]

[O]

[sh̲ower]

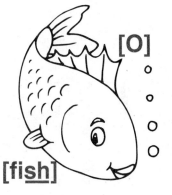

[O]

[fis̲h]

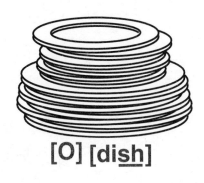

[O] [dis̲h]

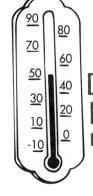

[G]
[t̲hermo-
meter]

[O] [sh̲ip]

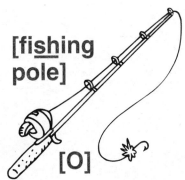

[fis̲hing
pole]

[O]

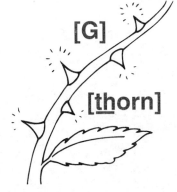

[G]

[t̲horn]

[G]   [Eart̲h]

PHONICS SKILLS

►Consonant Sounds and Spelling

Directions: Fill in the blanks with the correct letters to spell the words that match the pictures.

1.

cru __ t c h

2.

lun __ c h

3.

__ c h ___ icken

4.

ca __ t c h

▶ Sounds and Spelling

Directions: Circle the pictures that contain the /ar/ sound.

[car]

[cart]

[garden]

[party hats]

[starfish]

[dart]

[armor]

[arm]

[harp]

[marbles]

▶Review

Directions: Read each sentence. Write the correct word to complete each sentence.

PHONICS SKILLS

stack	shell	dock
jump	sled	lift

1. Jan helps Ted __stack__ the logs.

2. I cannot __lift__ this big box.

3. Lots of frogs __jump__ into that pond.

4. Ann sees a __shell__ in the sand.

5. Art likes to __sled__ down the hill.

6. Ships stop at the __dock__.

Review • Challenge: Phonics Skills

▶ Sounds and Spelling

Directions: Color red the items that begin with /w/. Color blue the items that begin with /hw/.

PHONICS SKILLS

[R]
[window]

[R]

[whale]
[B]

[windmill]

[R]
[water]

[B]
[wheel]

[walrus]
[R]

[wizard]
[R]

[well]
[R]

[R] [worm]
[R]
[watermelon]

PHONICS SKILLS

▶Vowel Sounds and Spelling

1.

b u r n

burn

2.

st i r

stir

3.

sh i r t

shirt

4.

t u r nip

turnip

5.

d i r t

dirt

6.

h u r t

hurt

UNIT 4 Our Neighborhood at Work • **Lesson 1** *Unit Introduction*

▶Review

Directions: Circle with a blue crayon the pictures whose names have the /a/ sound. Circle with a red crayon the pictures whose names have the /i/ sound. Circle with a green crayon the pictures whose names have the /o/ sound.

[B-hat]

[R-pin]

[B-badge]

[G-frog]

[G-dog]

[B-crab]

[G-clock]

[R-bib]

[R-lips]

Challenge: Phonics Skills • *Review*

► **Consonant Sounds and Spelling**

Directions: Color green the pictures whose names begin with /k/ spelled k. Then, write these words in the first column. Write the words ending with /k/ spelled ■ck or k in the second column.

PHONICS SKILLS

| kettle | kitten | chick | shark |

Starts with *k*

Ends with _*ck* or *k*

kettle

chick

kitten

shark

▶ Sounds and Spelling

Directions: Color the things in the picture that have the /ng/ sound.

[c]
[c]
[c]
[wings]
[spring]
[c]
[ring]
[c]
[sing]
[c]
[c]
[king]
[c]
[swing]
[c]
[string]
[c]
[gong]

PHONICS SKILLS

▶ Consonant Sounds and Spelling

Directions: Write the words that have the /kw/ sound spelled *qu___* on the quilt.

| quack | quilt | fuzz | squirm | splat |
| quick | push | quit | thick | squirrel |

PHONICS SKILLS

quack   quilt

quick   quit

squirrel   squirm

　Consonant Sounds and Spelling • Challenge: Phonics Skills

▶ Consonant Sounds and Spelling

Directions: Fill in the missing words to complete the sentences. Then, fill in the puzzle using the words you wrote.

PHONICS SKILLS

backyard   yarn   yanked   yams

ACROSS

1. The dog is in the

b a c k y a r d.

2. Tim y a n k e d the string.

DOWN

3. Jan likes y a m s.

4. The y a r n was tangled.

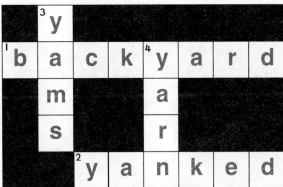

PHONICS SKILLS

▶Review

Directions: Circle the word that matches each picture and write it on the line. Then, write a sentence using one of the words.

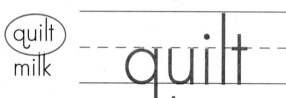

(quilt)
milk

quilt

(swing)
ring

swing

snack
(quack)

quack

(yarn)
yard

yarn

Sentence will vary.

▶ Vowel Sounds and Spelling

Directions: Look at each pair of words and write the one that contains the /ā/ sound.

1.   name   man

name

2.   ham   late

late

3.   tale   scar

tale

4.   bar   shade

shade

5.   grade   map

grade

6.   game   can

game

PHONICS SKILLS

▶ Consonant Sounds and Spelling

Directions: Write the correct word from the box next to each picture.

face	cent	circus	circle

1.

circle

2.

circus

3.

face

4.

cent

▶Review

Directions: Write the missing letter for each word. Then match the words to the pictures.

fa __C__ e

ca __K__ e

ra __C__ e

ca __P__ e

Name ______________________________ Date __________

PHONICS SKILLS

▶Vowel Sounds and Spelling

Directions: Circle the things whose names contain the /ī/ sound.

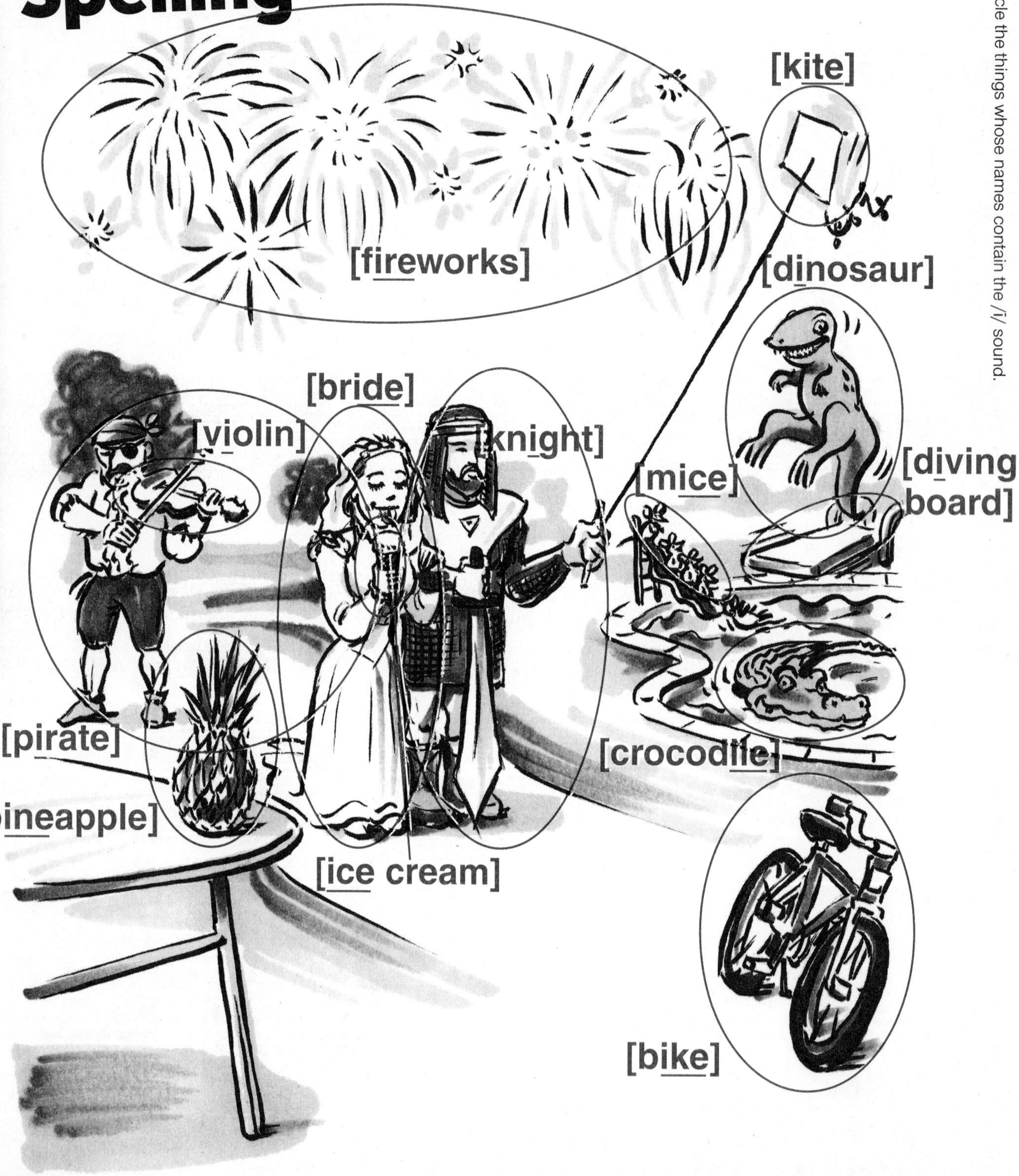
[kite]
[fireworks]
[dinosaur]
[bride]
[violin]
[knight]
[mice]
[diving board]
[pirate]
[crocodile]
[pineapple]
[ice cream]
[bike]

▶Sounds and Spelling

| rope | bone | note | nose | robe |

Directions: Find the picture for each word and circle it in red. Then write the words on the lines provided.

rope   robe

bone   nose

note

▶Review

PHONICS SKILLS

Directions: Color the six hidden objects in the picture. Then fill in the missing letters for each object.

b i k e   r a k e   k i t e

b o n e   p i p e   r o p e

Review • Challenge: Phonics Skills

▶Review

Directions: Complete the story by writing in the correct words on each line. You may use some words more than once and others not at all.

nine	rice	hike	lake	rope

I went on a  hike by the

 lake . I saw  nine

little birds in a nest. After the  hike ,

I ate  rice for lunch.

Challenge: Phonics Skills • *Review*   UNIT 4 • Lesson 13   **59**

PHONICS SKILLS

▶Consonant Sounds and Spelling

| van | drives | curve | save | five |

Directions: Complete the sentences. Then use those words to fill in the puzzle.

ACROSS

2. A ___curve___ is round.

3. Four plus one is ___five___.

4. I will ___save___ what I don't eat.

DOWN

1. Check the map as he ___drives___.

5. Jim drives a ___van___.

▶Vowel Sounds and Spelling

Directions: Color the items blue that contain the /ū/ sound.

[B]
[mule]

[B]
[menu]

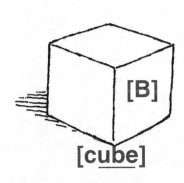
[B]
[cube]

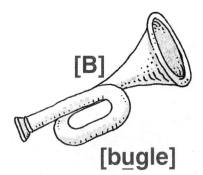
[B]
[bugle]

PHONICS SKILLS

▶Consonant Sounds and Spelling

Directions: Color the items that have /j/ spelled ge or gi.

[c]
[garage]

[c]
[giant]

[giraffe]

[genie]

[c]

[c]
[cage]

[c]
[gerbil]

[g]
[gem]

▶ Vowel Sounds and Spelling

Directions: Write the words containing the /ē/ and /e/ sound in the appropriate columns.

Steve	rest	athlete	bent
he	she	left	pet

E e

Steve   rest

athlete   bent

he   left

she   pet

PHONICS SKILLS

Directions: Circle the sentence that tells about each picture. Then, write the sentence on the line.

PHONICS SKILLS

▶Review

1.

(She has a large gem.)
The gem fell on her lap.

She has a large gem.

2.

(Steve rode the mule.)
The mule ate his hat.

Steve rode the mule.

3.

I can cut the vine.
(I swing on the vine.)

I swing on the vine.

▶Review

PHONICS SKILLS

▶ Vowel Sounds and Spelling

PHONICS SKILLS

steel	seat	teach	sea	leap

ACROSS
1 strong metal
4 chair

DOWN
2 to instruct
3 jump
4 ____ otter

UNIT 5 **Weather • Lesson 6** *Listen to the Rain*

▶Vowel Sounds and Spelling

Directions: Write the word that completes each sentence. Then, draw a picture of Trudy's birthday based on the sentences.

| happy | tiny | party | only | Trudy |

1. I went to a birthday __party__.

2. It was for my sister __Trudy__.

3. She got a __tiny__ cat.

4. The cat is __only__ six inches tall.

5. We were __happy__.

PHONICS SKILLS

▶**Sounds and Spelling**

PHONICS SKILLS

care	fare	chore
spare	year	wore

1. Jack __wore__ his tan pants.

2. Next __year__ we can go to camp.

3. We will take good __care__ of the cats.

4. What is the __fare__ to ride the bus?

5. Dad put the __spare__ tire in the trunk.

6. Dusting is a __chore__.

UNIT 5   Weather • **Lesson 8** *How's the Weather?*

▶ Vowel Sounds and Spelling

ai___
___ay

PHONICS SKILLS

may	talk	trim	(way)
mail	pop	(nail)	I
day	(say)	rich	fork
hail	city	(sail)	hat
train	ran	trip	(rain)
bay	(hay)	bat	tap

►Vowel Sounds and Spelling

Directions: Write the word that goes with each picture. Then, write the word that correctly completes each sentence.

PHONICS SKILLS

night	high	light

light   night   high

flight	fight	bright	tight

Her dress is **bright** pink.

This hat is too **tight** for me.

When is the next **flight** to Orlando?

The dogs got into a **fight**.

UNIT 5 **Weather • Lesson 10** *Clouds, Rain, Snow, and Ice*

▶ Review

PHONICS SKILLS

1. deal   real   seal   (cats)

2. (seek)   light   bright   night

3. nail   tail   (light)   pail

4. (fight)   pony   rainy   windy

5. ponies   (hay)   cities   pennies

cats seek light

fight hay

UNIT 5 Weather • **Lesson 11** *A Good Day for Kites*

▶Vowel Sounds and Spelling

Directions: Circle the six words that appear in the puzzle. The words appear horizontally and vertically.

___y
___ie

shy   pie   tie   sky   sly   why

S S H Y   S W

L P I E   K H

Y T I E   Y Y

▶ Vowel Sounds and Spellings

Directions: Color orange the things that have the /ō/ sound spelled _oe. Then write a sentence to describe something in the scene.

[O]
[JOE]

[O]
[toe]

WHEAT

[O]
[hoe]

Sentence will vary.

▶ Vowel Sounds and Spelling

Directions: Write the word that matches each picture.

PHONICS SKILLS

| bow | toaster | own | toad | road |

1.  toad

2.  road

3.  toaster

4.  own

5.  bow

UNIT 5 Weather • **Lesson 14** *Hurricanes*

▶ Vowel Sounds and Spelling

Directions: Circle the words that have the /ū/ sound. Then use one or two of them in sentences.

_ew
_ue

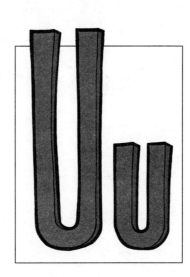

(few)	bird	turtle
(rescue)	city	(mew)
quiz	(pew)	skunk
cone	(argue)	(value)

Sentences will vary.

_____

— — — — — — — — — — — — — — — — — — — —

_____

— — — — — — — — — — — — — — — — — — — —

_____

▶Review

Directions: Circle in orange the words that have the /ō/ sound spelled oa, _ow. Circle in blue the words that have the /ū/ sound spelled _ue, _ew. Circle in green the words that have the /ī/ sound spelled _ie, _y.

 boat
[orange]

 argue
[blue]

 try
[green]

 tie
[green]

 pie
[green]

 crow
[orange]

 few
[blue]

 throat
[orange]

 fly
[green]

 cue
[blue]

 sky
[green]

 toad
[orange]

 show
[orange]

 mew
[blue]

 bow
[orange]

 rescue
[blue]

PHONICS SKILLS

▶ Vowel Sounds and Spelling

[balloon]

[goose]

[flute]

[jewels]

[rooster]

[ruler]

[June]

Be Back Soon
[soon]

Stew
[stew]

PHONICS SKILLS

PHONICS SKILLS

Directions: Draw in the items listed in the box. Write the names of the objects on the lines.

▶Vowel Sounds and Spelling

| football | hooks | books | cook |

[football] [cook] [hooks] [books]

football

books

hooks

cook

Vowel Sounds and Spelling • **Challenge: Phonics Skills**

▶ Decoding

Directions: Circle the words that have the /o͞o/ sound.

song   (loose)   tub   truck

(tube)   lost   (flew)   cost

son   (blue)   (soon)   store

(pool)   pail   (blew)   back

PHONICS SKILLS

▶Vowel Sounds and Spelling

Directions: Find the picture for each word and circle it in red. Then, write the words on the lines provided.

gown	owl	crown	clown	cow	flower

gown   owl   crown

clown   cow   flower

▶ Vowel Sounds and Spelling

Directions: Find the picture for each word and circle it in red. Then, write the words on the lines provided.

| cloud | mouse | blouse | trout | house | hound |

cloud mouse blouse

trout house hound

▶Vowel Sounds and Spelling

PHONICS SKILLS

1. (Our) (town) likes to see the circus.

2. A huge (crowd) gathers (outside) the big top.

3. The man in charge (bows) and (shouts) to us.

4. A (clown) with a big, red (mouth) leads us inside.

▶ Vowel Sounds and Spelling

Directions: Color the sections of the flower that have words containing the /aw/ sound. Then, write these words on the lines provided.

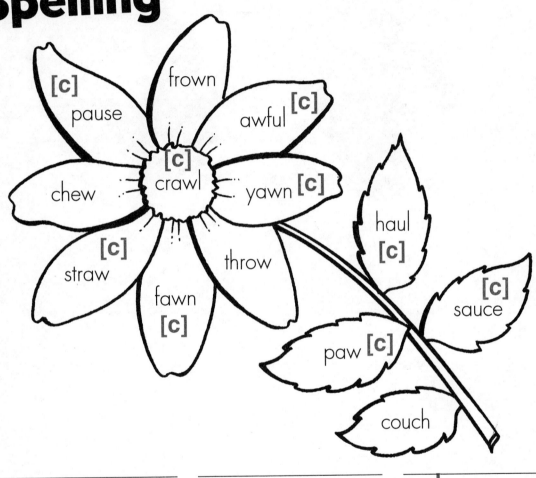

[c] pause
frown
awful **[c]**
[c] crawl
chew
yawn **[c]**
haul **[c]**
[c] straw
throw
[c] sauce
fawn **[c]**
paw **[c]**
couch

sauce   paw   haul

pause   yawn   fawn

awful   straw   crawl

▶ **Review**

Directions: Connect the dots in numerical order. Read each completed word aloud, then write the words on the lines. On the last line, write the name of what you see when all the dots are connected.

PHONICS SKILLS

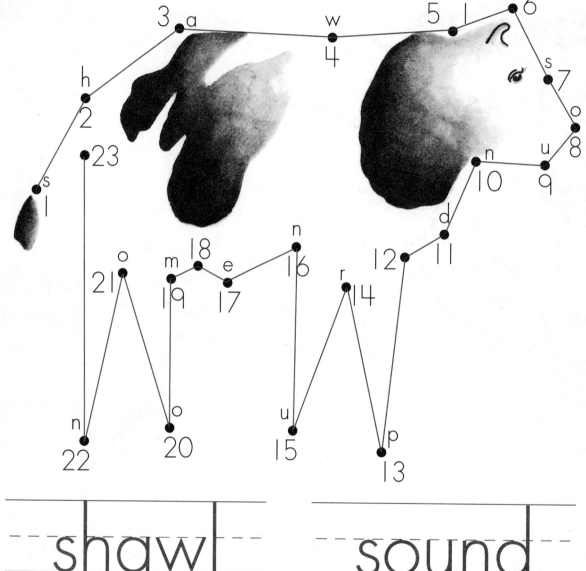

shawl   sound

prune   moon

cow

▶ Sounds and Spelling

Directions: Draw a line that connects each word with its picture. Then, write the words on the lines provided.

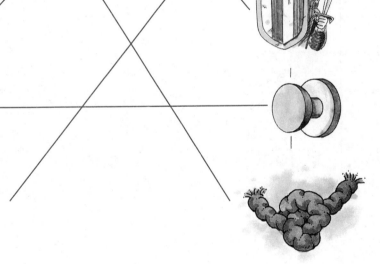

1. knight

2. knot

3. knee

4. knife

5. knob

6. knock

knight knot knee

knife knob knock

▶Review

Directions: Circle the word in each row that has the same vowel sound as the first word in the row.

PHONICS SKILLS

loop	book	wool	(boot)
took	spook	(look)	stool
food	good	(tool)	cook
shook	tool	(book)	pool
cool	(fool)	cookie	hook

▶ Word Endings: -er, -est

Directions: Read each group of sentences. Write the word on the line to correctly complete each sentence.

swift	swifter	swiftest

1. Carl's boat is ___ swifter ___ than Jed's.

2. Jane has a ___ swift ___ boat.

3. Mark's boat is the ___ swiftest ___.

old	older	oldest

4. Cosmo is ___ older ___ than Sassy.

5. Fido is the ___ oldest ___ dog of all.

6. Sassy is an ___ old ___ dog.

PHONICS SKILLS

▶Vowel Sounds and Spelling

Directions: Find your way through the maze. Follow the pictures whose names contain the /oi/ sound.

[coins]

[point]

[toys]

[boy]

[oil]

Vowel Sounds and Spelling • Challenge: Phonics Skills

UNIT 6   Journeys • **Lesson 13** *Our Class Trip*

▶Consonant Sounds and Spelling

Directions: Find the words from the box in the puzzle and circle them.

wrist	wrench	wrap	wrong	wreck	write

Q W M N Q P W R I S T

W R I T E A B B C D E

V E N W Q H A W J B A

S N W R O N G R H O B

M C L A H F J E A D C

T H R P P M X C R T F

P I D W U Y O K P U K

▶**Sounds and Spelling**

Directions: Draw a line connecting each word with its picture. Then, write a sentence on the lines provided using one of the words.

PHONICS SKILLS

1. trophy

2. phone

3. elephant

4. gopher

5. dolphin

6. pheasant

Sentences will

vary.

▶Review

The dolphin likes to rest.

(The dolphin jumps.)

The dolphin jumps.

(She digs in the soil.)

She got soil on her dress.

She digs in the soil.

(Pups like to wrestle.)

We wrestle on a mat.

Pups like to wrestle.

PHONICS SKILLS

UNIT 7 Keep Trying • **Lesson 2** *The Itsy Bitsy Spider*

▶Vowel Sounds and Spelling

▶**Use the words to complete the puzzle.**

dish	sun	tape	dock
no	pick	yes	day
wet	deep	show	cube

ACROSS
1. The ___ is shining.
3. The cat food is in the ___.
4. What ___ is it today?
6. We got ___ in the rain.
8. Did you ___ up your pen?
9. I put an ice ___ in my tea.

DOWN
1. Did you ___ the video?
2. ___, do not do it.
3. The pond is ___.
4. My boat is at the ___.
5. ___, you may go home.
7. I will ___ the box shut.

▶o Other than Short/Long o

▶**Read the words in the box. Write the word that matches each clue.**

done	dove	won	son	from	come

PHONICS SKILLS

1. the opposite of "lost" _____ won

2. to be finished _____ done

3. the opposite of "go" _____ come

4. a bird of peace _____ dove

5. a male child _____ son

6. the opposite of "to" _____ from

▶-alk and -all

▶ Write the name of the picture in the correct column.

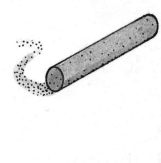

-all	**-alk**
ball	stalk
small	talk
tall	chalk

UNIT 7 Keep Trying • **Lesson 8** *74th Street*

▶Compare /o͞o/ and /u̅/

▶ **Match the vowel sounds. Write the name of each picture in the correct column.**

o͞o	**u̅**
spoon	mule
stool	bugle
hoop	cube
food	music

▶Phonics

Use the words to complete the puzzle.

PHONICS

saucer   taught   sauce   pause
laundry   applause   caught

ACROSS

2 the wash
3 did catch
5 clapping
7 stop for a moment

DOWN

1 served on food
4 did teach
6 dish

▶Reading and Writing

Write a story. Use the words in the box.

giant	gentle	cage	got
cottage	green	garden	give	grow

Answers will vary.

▶ Phonics

Write the word that matches each picture.
Then write a sentence about the picture.

wash	lamb	comb	crumb

1. comb

Sentences will vary.

2. crumb

3. wash

4. lamb

▶ Phonics

Answer the clues. Use the words in the box.

Complete the puzzle.

dive	flight	dread	bright	white
light	bread	feather	read	dead

ACROSS

2. a bird's _____
4. a plane _____
6. not living
9. a _____ light
10. rhymes with bread

DOWN

1. _____ snowflakes
3. _____ a book
5. sun _____
7. jump into water
8. _____ and butter

Challenge: Phonics Skills • /ī/ Spellings, /e/ Spelled ea

▶Phonics

PHONICS SKILLS

Write the word that matches each clue.

fuel	amuse	mule	cube
few	music	bugle	huge

1. what you sing — *music*

2. ice has this shape — *cube*

3. part horse, part donkey — *mule*

4. a horn — *bugle*

5. not many — *few*

6. what makes a car go — *fuel*

7. very big — *huge*

8. to make someone happy — *amuse*

▶Reading and Writing

Write the word that matches each picture. Then write a sentence about each picture.

pool	tooth	wood	zoo

1. wood

Sentences will vary.

2. tooth

3. pool

4. zoo

PHONICS SKILLS

▶ Phonics

Write the word that matches each clue.

| fire | fair | shore | store |
| deer | sore | picture | hear |

1. It's a place to shop. _____store_____

2. Smile and say "cheese" when someone takes this. _____picture_____

3. It's bright and hot. _____fire_____

4. It's where the sea meets the land. _____shore_____

5. It runs in the woods. _____deer_____

6. It has rides and games. _____fair_____

7. You use your ears to do this. _____hear_____

8. When your throat hurts, it is this. _____sore_____

UNIT 10 Homes • **Lesson I** *Unit Introduction*

▶Phonics Answer the clues. Use the words in the box. Complete the puzzle.

handle   table   edge   twice   slice   glance
change   candle   ice   cage   giant   rattle   bugle

ACROSS
1 a baby's toy
3 bird's house
5 horn
7 used to hold on to something
8 side
11 look quickly
12 two times

DOWN
2 what you eat on
3 money you get back
4 cut
6 gives off light
9 big person
10 frozen water

Challenge: Phonics Skills • *Vowel Spellings; Soft g and c*   UNIT 10 • Lesson I   **103**

▶ Phonics

▶ Write the word that matches each
picture. Then write a sentence about
each picture.

PHONICS

| honey   money   turkey   monkey |

1.  honey

Sentences will vary.

2. turkey

_____

3. monkey

_____

4. money

_____

▶Phonics

▶**Read the story. Underline the words that are spelled wrong. Write these words correctly in the spaces below.**

The County Fair

This is the <u>locashun</u> of the county fair. A <u>millyun</u> people will attend over the next two weeks. Some families take <u>vacashun</u> and go to the fair. The man at the gate will answer any <u>questyun</u> you may have. The rides are in full <u>moshun</u>. All kinds of food are sold. There is plenty of <u>acshun</u> at the fair.

location   question

million   motion

vacation   action

PHONICS